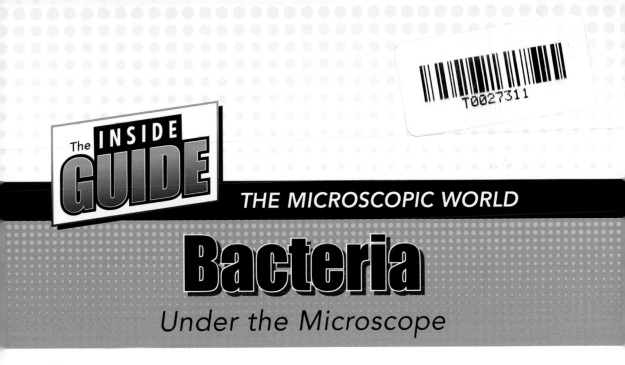

The INSIDE GUIDE

THE MICROSCOPIC WORLD

Bacteria

Under the Microscope

By Simon Pierce

Cavendish Square

Published in 2024 by Cavendish Square Publishing, LLC
2544 Clinton Street, Buffalo, NY 14224

Website: cavendishsq.com

This publication represents the opinions and views of the author based on their personal experience, knowledge, and research. The information in this book serves as a general guide only. The author and publisher have used their best efforts in preparing this book and disclaim liability rising directly or indirectly from the use and application of this book.

Disclaimer: Portions of this work were originally authored by Greg Roza and published as *Bacteria Up Close* (Under the Microscope). All new material this edition authored by Simon Pierce.

All websites were available and accurate when this book was sent to press.

Library of Congress Cataloging-in-Publication Data

Names: Pierce, Simon, author.
Title: Bacteria under the microscope / Simon Pierce.
Description: Buffalo, NY : Cavendish Square Publishing, [2024] | Series: The inside guide. The microscopic world | Includes bibliographical references and index.
Identifiers: LCCN 2022052319 | ISBN 9781502667878 (library binding) | ISBN 9781502667861 (paperback) | ISBN 9781502667885 (ebook)
Subjects: LCSH: Bacteria–Juvenile literature. | Microorganisms–Juvenile literature. | Microscopy–Juvenile literature.
Classification: LCC QR74.8 .P54 2024 | DDC 579.3–dc23/eng/20221223
LC record available at https://lccn.loc.gov/2022052319

Editor: Jennifer Lombardo
Copyeditor: Danielle Haynes
Designer: Deanna Paternostro

The photographs in this book are used by permission and through the courtesy of: Cover Stastny_Pavel/Shutterstock.com; p. 4 NYgraphic/Shutterstock.com; p. 6 Sherry V Smith/Shutterstock.com; p. 7 Vital9s/Shutterstock.com; p. 8 Stock-Asso/Shutterstock.com; p. 9 Everett Collection/Shutterstock.com; p. 10 nobeastsofierce/Shutterstock.com; p. 12 OSweetNature/Shutterstock.com; p. 13 Designua/Shutterstock.com; p. 15 Ducksoup/Wikimedia Commons; p. 16 Alexander Raths/Shutterstock.com; p. 18 Microspectacular/Shutterstock.com; p. 19 File Upload Bot (Magnus Manske)/Wikimedia Commons; p. 21 Lorcel/Shutterstock.com; p. 22 fizkes/Shutterstock.com; p. 24 Prostock-studio/Shutterstock.com; p. 25 america365/Shutterstock.com; p. 27 vchal/Shutterstock.com; p. 28 (top) GreenCam1/Shutterstock.com; p. 28 (bottom) MiniStocker/Shutterstock.com; p. 29 (top) Niphon Subsri/Shutterstock.com; p. 29 (bottom) Tatjana Baibakova/Shutterstock.com.

Some of the images in this book illustrate individuals who are models. The depictions do not imply actual situations or events.

CPSIA compliance information: Batch #CSCSQ24: For further information contact Cavendish Square Publishing LLC at 1-877-980-4450.

Printed in the United States of America

Find us on

CONTENTS

Bacteria and other germs can be spread when people touch their faces and then touch something else, such as a doorknob or phone. People don't touch things as much with their elbows, so sneezing or coughing into your elbow can help stop the spread.

DISCOVERING BACTERIA

Think about the last time you washed your hands or covered your nose and mouth before a sneeze. Today, we know we need to do these things to avoid spreading our germs to other people. However, in the past, people didn't know that. In fact, people didn't even know germs existed for most of human history.

In the distant past, humans did a lot of things to stay healthy without really knowing why those things worked. For example, humans learned early on that they needed to go to the bathroom far away from where they cooked their food. They knew it would make the food smell and taste bad, and that people would start to get sick before too long—although they didn't know exactly why that would happen. It wasn't until the mid-1600s that people started to discover germs. The first kind of germ scientists identified was bacteria.

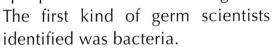

Fast Fact

A germ makes people sick. Certain kinds of bacteria, viruses, fungi, and **protozoa** are considered germs.

An Important Tool

The tool that made the discovery of bacteria possible was the microscope. The first microscope was made in 1590 when Dutch lens

One of the reasons we bury our dead is because disease-causing bacteria grow on the bodies.

makers put two lenses inside a tube. Scientists, including Galileo Galilei, experimented with lenses and made great improvements to microscopes. These improvements made it possible to see things as small as bacteria. Because bacteria are both microscopic and alive, people who study them are called microbiologists. Biology is a branch of science that deals with living things and how they work.

Fast Fact

The first microscope could only magnify objects about 10 times. However, the most powerful microscopes today can magnify objects up to 20 million times.

EARLY IDEAS ABOUT DISEASE

Before the invention of the microscope, people came up with all kinds of ideas about how diseases were spread. Many ancient societies believed that sickness was a punishment from the gods.

Over time, people decided that diseases came not from the gods, but from things around them, such as bad smells. Early theories, or ideas, sometimes led to dangerous, or unsafe, practices. For example, sometimes doctors thought a person was sick because they had too much blood in their body. A practice called bloodletting drained some of the patient's blood. Bloodletting doesn't cure any disease, and the practice itself can kill people.

Bloodsucking animals called leeches (*shown here*) were used for bloodletting for many years.

Today, microscopes are an important part of many branches of science.

Dutch scientist Antonie van Leeuwenhoek is sometimes called "the father of microbiology." During the 1660s, van Leeuwenhoek became interested in making lenses as a hobby. His first microscopes were nothing more than very powerful magnifying lenses.

Van Leeuwenhoek magnified many things with his microscopes, including **pond scum**, rainwater, and well water. In 1676, he was shocked to find tiny creatures living in these and other sources—including his own mouth! Van Leeuwenhoek had discovered bacteria. However, they weren't given a name until 1838. That year, German scientist

Christian Gottfried Ehrenberg came up with the word "bacterium." This is what we call just one of these creatures. "Bacteria" is the plural form of the word.

More to Learn

After van Leeuwenhoek's discovery, people knew bacteria existed, but they didn't know much more than that. Many people believed bacteria and other microscopic creatures, or microorganisms, popped into existence when food spoiled. This was called the spontaneous generation theory.

In the late 1800s, a scientist named Louis Pasteur disproved spontaneous generation. He also came up with the germ theory of disease, which states that the spread of microorganisms can make people sick. People started learning much more about bacteria after that.

Fast Fact

Louis Pasteur developed a process of heating food to kill the bacteria in it and keep it from spoiling. Today, the pasteurization process is widely used to keep milk from spoiling.

Louis Pasteur's experiments made food much safer.

The long strands on this bacterium are called flagella.

Bacteria are single-celled organisms. Many are just 1 micrometer, or micron, long—that's just one-millionth of a meter! Some are smaller than that, and some are larger. Bacteria come in three main shapes. They can be round or oval shaped, rod shaped, or **spiral** shaped. Most, but not all, bacteria are capable of movement. Some use narrow, whiplike parts called flagella. Some can spin and turn. Others make a slime to glide around, somewhat like snails.

The names scientists give to different kinds of bacteria are based on their shape and the way they group together. Round bacteria are called cocci, rod-shaped bacteria are called bacilli, and spiral bacteria are called spirilla. **Prefixes** are used to describe bacteria joined together in groups. Diplo- describes a pair of bacteria. Bacteria in a cluster have the prefix staphylo-, and chains of bacteria have the prefix strepto-.

Fast Fact

Bacteria are some of the fastest creatures on Earth. Many can move 100 times their own body length in 1 second.

Prokaryotes

The single cell of a bacterium is a type called a prokaryote. This is different from human cells, which are called eukaryotes. Like human

Bacteria Shapes

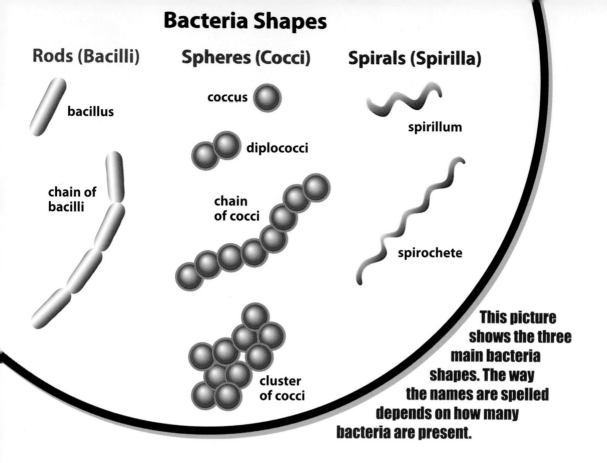

Rods (Bacilli)

bacillus

chain of bacilli

Spheres (Cocci)

coccus

diplococci

chain of cocci

cluster of cocci

Spirals (Spirilla)

spirillum

spirochete

This picture shows the three main bacteria shapes. The way the names are spelled depends on how many bacteria are present.

cells, prokaryotes have an outer membrane that protects their insides. Unlike in human cells, however, the parts of a prokaryote aren't surrounded by membranes. Instead, they float in a gel-like liquid called cytoplasm within the cell. Prokaryotes are the most common forms of life on Earth, and most are bacteria.

All living cells have genetic material called deoxyribonucleic acid (DNA). Genes are bits of DNA that determine the **traits** parents pass on to their offspring, or the children they make. In humans, this could be anything from hair color to earlobe shape.

DNA is packed in thread-like structures called chromosomes. In human cells, chromosomes are contained in the nucleus, which is somewhat like a cell's brain. In bacteria, chromosomes float freely

Difference between prokaryotic and eukaryotic cell

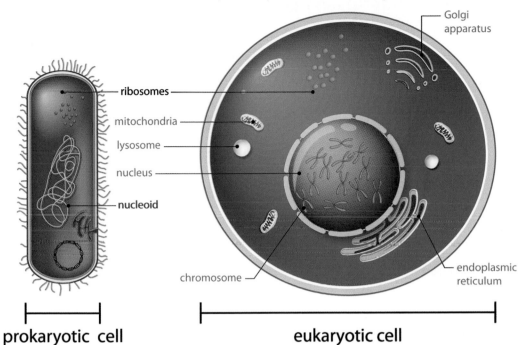

prokaryotic cell

eukaryotic cell

Take a look at these two cells, and see if you can spot all the differences between them.

in the main part of the cell, which is called the nucleoid.

Most bacteria are surrounded by an outer cell wall that protects them from their surroundings. Inside the cell wall is the cell membrane, which stops harmful chemicals from entering the cell. Inside the cell membrane, the bacterium's parts float freely in cytoplasm. The cytoplasm

Aerobes are microorganisms that use oxygen for growth and energy. Microorganisms called anaerobes don't need oxygen. Bacteria can be either aerobic or anaerobic.

HELPFUL BACTERIA

Some bacteria cause disease or make food spoil. Some do nothing to humans. However, some are so important to us that we need them to live. For example, without bacteria in our gut, we wouldn't be able to fully **digest** food!

Bacteria are also an important part of **fermentation**. This process is how we get alcohol, yogurt, sour cream, kombucha, and more. Fermented foods are sometimes called "probiotics" because they encourage the growth of good bacteria in the gut. People can also take probiotics as pills. Sometimes doctors will tell people to do this if they've recently taken antibiotics to stop an **infection**. An antibiotic can't tell the difference between helpful and harmful bacteria, so it kills them both.

holds important **enzymes** that help break down food and build cell parts. A bacterium also has stored **nutrients** and ribosomes. Ribosomes create the proteins needed for growth, repair, and other biological processes.

Fast Fact

In 2016, Japanese scientists discovered a type of bacterium that eats plastic. They're studying it to see if it could be helpful in getting rid of plastic pollution.

The first antibiotic, penicillin, was discovered by accident by Scottish scientist Alexander Fleming (shown here). When mold grew on the bacteria he was studying, he realized the mold had killed the bacteria. The mold was later used to create penicillin.

Soap and water is enough to kill most bacteria. However, for surfaces that are very dirty or for places that need to be very clean, such as a hospital, people use cleaning products such as these.

Chapter Three

BACTERIA ALL AROUND

Bacteria are everywhere around us. They aren't just in our bodies; they're also on every surface we touch, in the air, in the ground, and in the water. They reproduce very easily and very quickly. In fact, one species can double its numbers in as little as 4 minutes. If a single bacterium is given enough food, it can create a billion more cells just like itself in 10 hours! The ability to reproduce rapidly has helped bacteria survive for billions of years. In fact, this trait makes some harmful bacteria incredibly difficult to fight.

Fast Fact

Bacteria adapt to things very quickly. This is one reason why doctors don't use antibiotics to treat illnesses unless they have to. Any bacteria that aren't killed by the antibiotic adapt to resist it and become what we call "superbugs."

Making a Copy

Most bacteria can reproduce by themselves. Usually, a single bacterium splits into two new cells. This process is called binary fission. "Binary" means "having two parts." "Fission" is the act of splitting into different parts. When a bacterium undergoes binary fission, it

500 nm

HV
00 kV

Mag
8900 x

This photo, taken from under a microscope, shows cells undergoing binary fission.

grows to about twice its normal size. It makes an exact copy of its DNA. The cell membrane then grows down the middle of the cell, and each side gets its own genetic material.

Some bacteria reproduce through a process called budding. This occurs when a new cell, called a "daughter," grows on the side of a parent cell, called a "mother." The mother creates genetic material for the daughter. The daughter grows larger and then separates from the mother, resulting in a new cell.

Living Together

Because they multiply so quickly, most bacteria live in large groups known as colonies. Colonies can take on different forms

Some deep-sea fish, such as this dragonfish, have bacteria inside them that glow. This glow is called bioluminescence. The dragonfish uses this light to help it hunt for food.

Fast Fact

When bacteria that live in the soil feed on dead organisms, they break them down and release the nutrients locked in the organisms. Plants can then take those nutrients from the soil to help them grow.

EXTREMOPHILES

Bacteria are found everywhere on Earth's surface. Some, called extremophiles, can live in places that are too harsh for most living things to survive. They can survive in the frozen polar ice caps and in the near-boiling water of hot springs. Some live around volcanic vents on the ocean floor.

Bacteria can even survive in outer space! As far as we know, bacteria don't live there naturally. However, when astronauts go to space, they take bacteria with them. Even though the spacecraft are carefully cleaned, it's impossible to kill every single bacterium. When astronauts come back to Earth, their ships are often covered in bacteria and fungi. This shows that they can continue to live and grow in space.

depending on the species. Many group closely together in clusters. Others form long chains.

The substance in or on which a bacteria colony grows is called the growth medium. The more food available in the growth medium, the faster and bigger the colony will grow. In order to survive, bacteria need a source of food. Some bacteria make food the same way plants do—with sunlight, carbon dioxide, and water. Other bacteria make

The extremophiles that live in this hot spring in Yellowstone National Park give the water its beautiful colors.

enzymes and use them to break down outside matter into nutrients small enough to pass through their cell wall. Some even consume inorganic materials, such as sulfur and iron.

The largest known bacteria colonies are found in Earth's oceans. In 2010, scientists discovered a giant "mat" of bacteria in the Pacific Ocean off the coast of South America. This colony covers about the same amount of space as the country Greece!

Many of the **symptoms** people experience when they're fighting off a bacterial infection come from the immune system. For example, a fever can make the body too warm for bacteria to live in comfortably.

FIGHTING BACK

Most bacteria are either harmless or helpful to humans. Even when it comes to the bacteria that make us sick, the body's immune system can often fight off a bacterial infection. The immune system is made up of cells, tissues, and organs that work together to battle pathogens, or germs. When harmful bacteria enter the body, white blood cells work to destroy them. White blood cells produce substances called antibodies, which identify and bind to germs. Once this happens, other white blood cells called T cells destroy the harmful bacteria.

Some bacteria produce harmful substances called toxins that cause diseases. Toxins can be made by living bacteria or can be released when bacteria die. An antibody that binds to a toxin is called an antitoxin. Some bacteria normally found in the body can cause illnesses when they reproduce more quickly than the body can fight them off. Other species harm plants and animals on farms where we get our food.

Fast Fact

Sleep is an important part of keeping us healthy because that's when the immune system does most of its work. If a person gets fewer than five hours of sleep per night on a regular basis, they're much more likely to get sick.

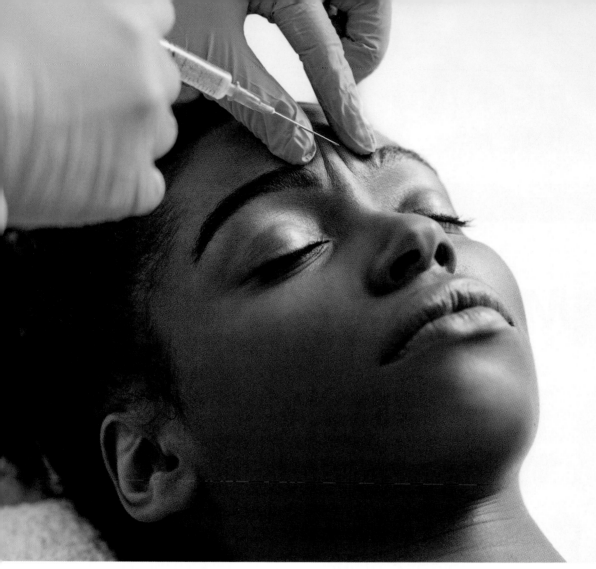

A bacterium called *Clostridium botulinum* creates a neurotoxin, or toxin that numbs the nerves. It's used in a treatment called Botox that can help get rid of wrinkles. It can also be found in spoiled food. Injecting this bacterium is safe, but eating it can be deadly.

Help from Medicine

When the body can't fight a bacterial infection on its own, a doctor can prescribe, or order, antibiotics. As the name suggests, antibiotics only

A SCARY INFECTION

Necrotizing fasciitis is an infection that causes necrosis (cell death) of the fascia (a layer of connective tissue beneath the skin). Several different kinds of bacteria can cause this disease. They're commonly known as "flesh-eating" bacteria. The bacteria usually enter the body through a wound and then reproduce rapidly. They make a toxin that destroys tissue very quickly.

Necrotizing fasciitis can be deadly; in fact, about 20 percent of all cases end in death. Victims who live are often left scarred or disabled. Fortunately, this infection is also very rare and can be treated if someone gets to a doctor right away.

A bacterium called *Vibrio vulnificus* can cause necrotizing fasciitis. It lives in warm, slightly salty pools of water. After Hurricane Ian hit Florida in September 2022, the state health department announced that floodwaters caused a huge increase in *V. vulnificus* infections.

work on bacteria. If an infection is caused by a different pathogen or if it's unclear what's causing it, doctors may not prescribe an antibiotic. It depends a lot on things such as how sick the patient is and what the infection is like. Making sure antibiotics are used only when they're really needed is good for two reasons. First, it means a patient doesn't waste time taking a medicine that won't help them. Second, it helps stop bacteria from turning into superbugs.

Bacterial Infections

Bacteria can cause many kinds of illnesses. Some are much more common than others. This has a lot to do with where people encounter bacteria. For example, a bacterium called *Burkholderia pseudomallei* causes a disease called melioidosis, or Whitmore's disease. This disease is very rare in the United States because the bacterium is mostly found in tropical places. In contrast, *Salmonella* causes about 1.35 million cases of food poisoning in the United States each year. It lives in birds and other animals. Since chicken and eggs are popular foods in America, the chance of getting salmonellosis—a type of food poisoning—from improperly prepared food is high compared to some other bacterial infections.

In some cases, people can protect themselves from a bacterial infection by getting a **vaccine**. This also stops people from spreading the infection.

Fast Fact

Mycobacterium tuberculosis causes an infection called tuberculosis. According to the World Health Organization (WHO), this disease is one of the top 10 causes of death around the world.

Eggs can be tested in a lab to see if they contain *Salmonella*. However, this is rarely done because only about 1 out of every 2,000 eggs has the bacterium in it. Infection is easy to avoid by thoroughly cooking anything that contains eggs.

Meningitis is one bacterial infection we have a vaccine for. It's very **contagious**, so many schools require people to get the vaccine before they can attend.

Fast Fact

There are more bacterial cells in your body than there are human cells. Most of these are good bacteria. Less than 1 percent of all the bacteria in the world are harmful to humans.

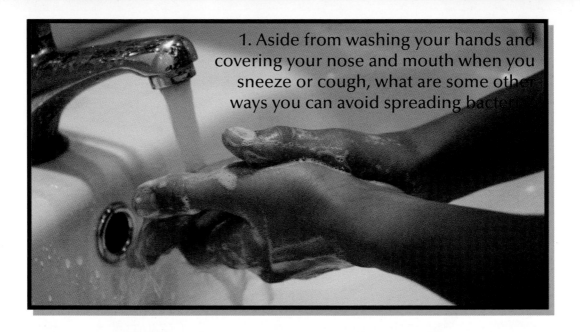

1. Aside from washing your hands and covering your nose and mouth when you sneeze or cough, what are some other ways you can avoid spreading bacteria?

2. What kinds of traits do you think bacteria pass on through their DNA?

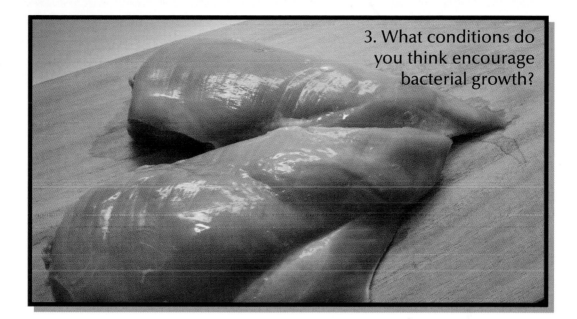

3. What conditions do you think encourage bacterial growth?

4. What can you do to boost your immune system?

GLOSSARY

contagious: Able to be passed from person to person.

digest: To break down food inside the body so the body can use it for energy and nutrients.

enzyme: A protein made in the body that helps chemical reactions occur.

fermentation: A process by which an organism changes a sugar or starch into an alcohol or acid in the absence of oxygen.

infection: A sickness caused by germs entering the body.

nutrient: Something taken in by a plant or animal that helps it grow and stay healthy.

pond scum: A mass of tangled threads of algae in still water.

prefix: A letter or group of letters that comes at the beginning of a word and has a meaning of its own.

protozoa: Single-celled, eukaryotic microorganisms.

spiral: A shape or line that curls outward from a center point.

symptom: A change in a living thing that indicates the presence of a disease or other physical disorder.

trait: A quality that makes one person or thing different from another.

vaccine: A drug often made from weakened or dead microorganisms that helps build up the immune system against a disease.

Books

Axelrod-Contrada, Joan. *Mini Mind Controllers: Fungi, Bacteria, and Other Tiny Zombie Makers*. North Mankato, MN: Capstone Press, 2021.

Levine, Sarah. *Germs Up Close*. Minneapolis, MN: Millbrook Press, 2021.

Mayer, Melissa. *The Micro World of Viruses and Bacteria*. North Mankato, MN: Capstone Press, 2022.

Websites

BrainPOP: Bacteria
www.brainpop.com/games/virtuallabsbacteriasampling
See what being a microbiologist is like in this interactive video.

Ducksters: Bacteria
www.ducksters.com/science/bacteria.php
Learn more about bacteria, and test your knowledge with a quick quiz.

Kiddle: Bacteria Facts for Kids
kids.kiddle.co/Bacteria
Read about how to stop the spread of bacteria, and take a look at some photos taken under a microscope.

INDEX